MW00460186

Planet POWER

by Hannah Sperber

Introduction

We use energy for lots of things. We use energy to light and heat our homes and power our computers and TVs. Energy is incredible.

Most of the energy that we consume today comes from **fossil fuels**, such as oil, gas, or coal. Fossil fuels come from the remains of plants and animals that lived millions of years ago. Burning fossil fuels releases energy.

smokestack

Burning fossil fuels such as coal pollutes the air.

turbine

Wind farms generate electricity to power about 9 million homes in the United States.

However, burning fossil fuels pollutes the air. Fossil fuels are also not renewable. They can only be used once. They will <u>run out</u> in the future.

Sun, water, and wind are renewable sources of energy. We can reuse renewable energy, and renewable energy does not pollute the air.

It is no coincidence that more people want to use renewable energy. We can use energy from the wind to power our homes. We can use energy from the sun to power cars and houses. We can use energy from water to produce electricity.

In Other Words to use something until there isn't any more. En español, *run out* quiere decir *acabar*.

CHAPTER 1

The Power of Water

People have always used water as a source of energy. People used the moving water in rivers and streams to turn waterwheels. The waterwheels were used to grind grains into flour.

Later, people built dams to make hydropower, or water power. The energy of the water from a dam **generates** electricity. The movement of the water turns machines called **turbines**. When the turbines move, they generate electricity.

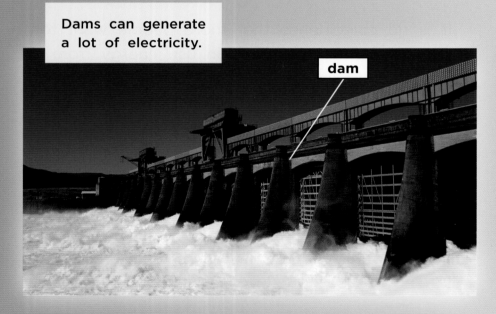

Dams can generate a lot of electricity.

dam

In the 1970s, there was an oil **crisis**. The supply of oil decreased, and there <u>was not</u> enough oil for people to use. A scientist named Stephen Salter looked for ways to use energy from ocean waves.

Salter and other scientists invented a machine called the Salter Duck. It moved up and down on the ocean waves. A turbine inside the Salter Duck converted each movement into electricity.

People thought the Salter Duck wouldn't survive storms in the ocean. Scientists worked to improve the Salter Duck.

Language Detective <u>Was not</u> is a negative. Find another example of a negative on this page.

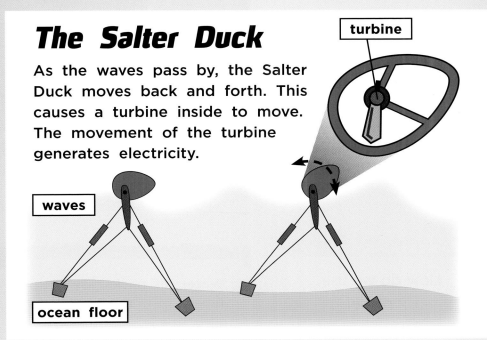

The Salter Duck

As the waves pass by, the Salter Duck moves back and forth. This causes a turbine inside to move. The movement of the turbine generates electricity.

turbine

waves

ocean floor

It is difficult to capture the energy of waves. Storms cause destructive winds and waves. When there is no wind, there are no waves.

However, people are working to improve ways to capture wave energy. The first commercial wave farm was built off the coast of Oregon in 2010. People want efficient and inexpensive wave energy.

Up, Up, and Away!

A jet pack allows a person to fly just like a superhero. Water jet packs are powered by water. They can lift a person into the air. A water jet pack can move at about 30 miles per hour.

jet pack

Water jet packs use the power of water to move.

STOP AND CHECK

How do we use water power?

CHAPTER 2

Heat from the Inside

Water, wind, and solar energy depend on the weather. Wind energy requires wind. There is no solar energy when the sun isn't shining. However, weather doesn't control **geothermal** energy.

Geothermal energy comes from the heat inside Earth. Some geothermal energy comes to the surface of Earth in geysers or hot springs. Thousands of years ago, people began using geothermal energy to cook, wash, and keep warm.

hot spring

Many hot springs are in volcanic areas. They release hot water from the ground.

People explored other ways to use geothermal energy in the nineteenth century.

Then in 1931, a plumber named Charlie Lieb used a hot-water well to heat a home in Oregon. Lieb installed pipes that were filled with water and went into the hot-water well. The water inside the pipes got hot, and the hot water flowed back into the house.

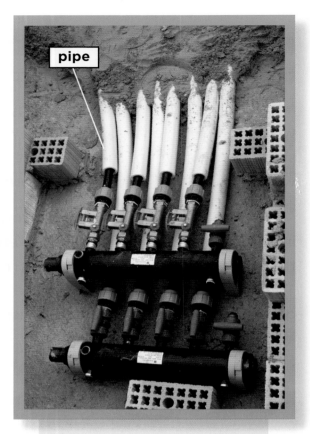

pipe

In a home that uses geothermal energy, pipes carry the heat from under the ground into the house.

Lieb's invention was an important development in geothermal heating systems.

These days, people use geothermal energy in all types of buildings, from homes, to schools and offices. Geothermal heating is efficient, clean, and less expensive than heating by using fossil fuels.

Geothermal systems in houses use heat pumps. In winter, heat from the ground travels through pipes to the heat pump. In summer, the heat pump removes the heat from the home and returns it to the ground.

STOP AND CHECK

How do people use geothermal energy?

A Home Geothermal Heating System

Heat travels from under the ground to the geothermal heat pump. The heat pump sends the warmed air through the house.

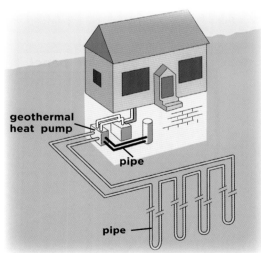

geothermal heat pump

pipe

pipe

CHAPTER 3

The Power of the Sun

Solar energy <u>doesn't</u> pollute the environment, and it is renewable. People have used the sun's energy since ancient times. The ancient Greeks built their homes to face the sun. The ancient Romans put glass in windows to trap the sun's heat.

Today some buildings have solar panels on their roofs. Solar panels trap the sun's rays and convert the energy in the sun's rays into heat or electricity.

Language Detective

Doesn't is a negative contraction. Find another example on page 7.

solar panel

The solar panels on this roof capture the sun's energy.

The Solar Challenger has solar panels on its wings.

Engineer Paul MacCready helped make an aircraft called the *Solar Challenger*. It was powered by the sun.

In 1981, the *Solar Challenger* flew 163 miles (262 kilometers) from France to England. The flight took about five and a half hours. The *Solar Challenger* set a world record for the longest solar-powered flight with a pilot.

Since then other solar aircraft have been built. These aircraft collect information to help scientists study the weather. The aircraft are controlled from Earth, and they don't have pilots.

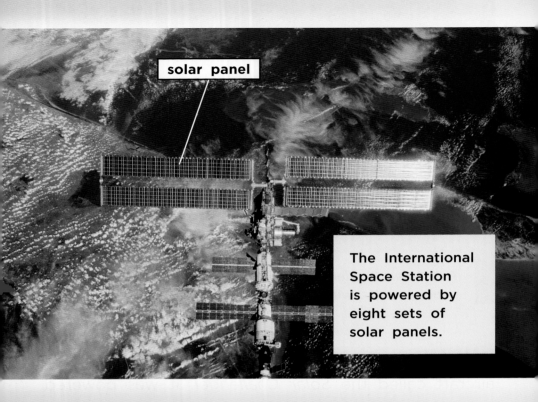

solar panel

The International Space Station is powered by eight sets of solar panels.

Solar energy can free machines from a regular power supply. In 1988, the International Space Station (ISS) was launched into space.

The station has to be self-sufficient because it isn't plugged into a regular power supply. Instead, the station runs on solar energy. It has solar panels along its wings. The solar panels absorb energy from the sun's rays. They generate electricity for the station.

Now scientists are exploring the possibility of using solar panels in space to power machines back on Earth.

Solar panels in space would generate solar energy all the time. Weather would not affect the solar panels in space. Scientists are exploring ways to send solar energy from space back to Earth in a safe and affordable way.

STOP AND CHECK

How can we use solar energy?

THE RACE IS ON!

Every two years, the United States Department of Energy runs the Solar Decathlon challenge. Teams of university students from around the world compete to build the best solar-powered house.

The teams work hard to design houses that use renewable energy. These houses could be built in the future.

Conclusion

One urgent problem we have is finding good energy sources. There are negative consequences of using nonrenewable resources, such as fossil fuels. Using fossil fuels causes pollution, and fossil fuel supplies are running out. People are looking for ways to use more renewable energy.

It will be a long time before we use renewable energy for all our needs. However, people are inventing new things all the time. <u>The future looks bright</u> for renewable energy!

> **In Other Words** it seems it will be successful in the future. En español, *the future looks bright* quiere decir *parece que tendrá éxito en el futuro.*

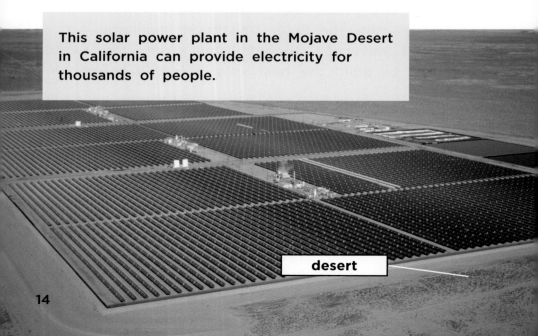

This solar power plant in the Mojave Desert in California can provide electricity for thousands of people.

desert

Respond to Reading

Summarize

Use important details to summarize *Planet Power.* Your graphic organizer may help you.

Main Idea
Detail
Detail
Detail

Text Evidence

1. How can you tell that *Planet Power* is informational text? **GENRE**

2. What is the main idea of the first paragraph on page 9? **MAIN IDEA AND KEY DETAILS**

3. The prefix *hydro-* means water. What does *hydropower* mean on page 4? Use context clues and the meaning of the prefix. **LATIN AND GREEK PREFIXES**

4. Write about how the International Space Station runs. Include key details from the text. **WRITE ABOUT READING**

Compare Texts
Read a Greek myth about the sun and how it moves across the sky.

Helios and Phaeton

Ancient Greeks believed in a powerful sun god named Helios. Helios glowed with orange and red light and energy.

Every morning, Helios came out of a cave below the ocean. He got on a golden chariot with four horses. Helios provided light all over Earth as he rode the chariot across the sky.

Helios

horse

Phaeton

One day, Helios saw his son Phaeton. Helios was happy to see Phaeton. "Welcome, Phaeton! What can I do for you?"

Phaeton replied, "I want to drive your golden chariot." Helios was horrified. Only Helios could drive the golden chariot. Not even Zeus, the ruler of all the gods, could drive the golden chariot. Helios explained that the horses breathed fire. They were very difficult to control. But Phaeton wouldn't listen.

Helios put oil on Phaeton's head to protect Phaeton from the heat. Phaeton took the horses' reins, but Phaeton couldn't control them.

The horses pulled the chariot up into space. Earth began to freeze. Then the horses plunged toward Earth. This started fires, and the oceans and rivers dried up.

Zeus threw a lightning bolt at the chariot to stop it. Phaeton fell out of the chariot, and Helios took the horses' reins again. Helios was the driver of the golden chariot again.

Make Connections

What does *Helios and Phaeton* tell you about how important the sun was for the ancient Greeks? **ESSENTIAL QUESTION**

Compare the importance of energy from the sun in ancient Greece to modern sources of energy. Why is the sun still so important? **TEXT TO TEXT**

Glossary

crisis an unstable time *(page 5)*

fossil fuels fuels such as oil, gas, and coal that were formed from living things a long time ago *(page 2)*

generates makes or produces *(page 4)*

geothermal having to do with heat from within Earth *(page 7)*

turbines machines that use flowing water, steam, or air to turn blades and produce electricity *(page 4)*

Index

Focus on Science

Purpose To make a solar-powered oven

Procedure

Step 1 With a partner, draw a rectangle 1 inch in from the edge of a shoebox lid. Cut out the rectangle.

Step 2 Cover the shoebox lid with a sheet of clear plastic. This is your oven window. Use masking tape to seal the edges of the window.

Step 3 Line the shoebox with aluminum foil. Wrap the foil over the top edge of each side. Put the lid on.

Step 4 Take the oven outside to a sunny spot. Use a thermometer to record the temperatures inside and outside the oven. Record the temperatures again in 20 minutes.

Conclusion How much did the temperature of your oven change? How much warmer or colder was it inside the oven compared to the outside? What kinds of things could you do with a solar oven?